This Recipe Finder-Tracking Guide belongs to:

_____

Get Outside and Garden!

64 Fun Gardening Ideas. These easy-to do projects will inspire both Experienced and Newbie Gardeners to go outside and play in the dirt! Gardening is good for your health, both physically and mentally. Statistics show that gardening and being out-doors reduces stress and has a calming effect on the mind. Gardening helps to give our lives meaning. It allows us to enter the transcendent state of mind where we experience inner wakefulness and great calm and peace.

Garden Planning & Record-Keeping Workbook

This may prove to be the most useful gardening book in your library. You have a constant flow of ideas and questions about the outdoor areas surrounding your home. But other issues often claim your time, and things in your yard some-times get pushed aside or forgotten until the season, or the correct timing for the activity, has passed. This book will help to ensure that things get done in a timely manner. Inside, you will create a season-to-season and year-to-year record of all the happenings in your garden. It's your depository for your plans and dreams for your garden areas.

My Recipe Finder-Tracking Guide

Jean Boles

My Recipe Finder-Tracking Guide
Copyright © 2017 Jean Boles

Boles
Books
Publishing

ISBN: 978-1541233171

Printed in the United States of America

*An easy way to keep track of your favorite recipes
from the cookbooks in your library*

Contents

Introduction

"Home cooking is the true embodiment of love. It makes us show patience, kindness, humility, hope, and perseverance."
— Agus Ekanurdi, *Cook Your Way to Love & Harmony*

How many times have you leafed through your cookbooks and dog-eared pages containing enticing recipes, only to later forget about them. If you have more than one or two cookbooks, you may never remember to go back to that particular cookbook and try out that recipe. Now, with this *Recipe Finder-Tracking Guide*, you can jot down the name of the cookbook in which you found that taste-tempting recipe that you want to try, the page number in that cookbook and the name of the recipe. You will place this note under the proper heading—meats, vegetables, desserts, etc.—where you can easily find it when you are ready to prepare it for your family. Afterwards, you can rate it in the Finder-Tracker Guide for future reference. So track down those recipes, jot down the cookbook links and get cookin'!

"The only real stumbling block is fear of failure. In cooking you've got to have a what-the-hell attitude."
— Julia Child

Appetizers

Name of Recipe

_____

Name of Cookbook   *Page number*

_____

Date first prepared _____

Rate this recipe: Excellent ____ Good ____ Average____

Additional Comments _____

_____

_____

Name of Recipe

_____

Name of Cookbook   *Page number*

_____

Date first prepared _____

Rate this recipe: *Excellent* ____ *Good* ____ *Average* ____

Additional Comments _____

_____

_____

━━

Name of Recipe

_____

Name of Cookbook   *Page number*

_____

Date first prepared _____

Rate this recipe: *Excellent* ____ *Good* ____ *Average* ____

Additional Comments _____

_____

_____

Name of Recipe

_____

Name of Cookbook   *Page number*

_____

Date first prepared _____

Rate this recipe: Excellent ____ *Good* ____ *Average* ____

Additional Comments _____

_____

_____

━━

Name of Recipe

_____

Name of Cookbook   *Page number*

_____

Date first prepared _____

Rate this recipe: Excellent ____ *Good* ____ *Average* ____

Additional Comments _____

_____

_____

Name of Recipe
_____

Name of Cookbook   *Page number*
_____

Date first prepared _____

Rate this recipe: *Excellent* ___ *Good* ___ *Average* ___

Additional Comments _____
_____
_____

═══════════════════════════════

Name of Recipe
_____

Name of Cookbook   *Page number*
_____

Date first prepared _____

Rate this recipe: *Excellent* ___ *Good* ___ *Average* ___

Additional Comments _____
_____
_____

Name of Recipe

_____

Name of Cookbook   *Page number*

_____

Date first prepared _____

Rate this recipe: Excellent ___ *Good* ___ *Average* ___

Additional Comments _____

_____

_____

Name of Recipe

_____

Name of Cookbook   *Page number*

_____

Date first prepared _____

Rate this recipe: Excellent ___ *Good* ___ *Average* ___

Additional Comments _____

_____

_____

Soups

Name of Recipe

_____

Name of Cookbook   *Page number*

_____

Date first prepared _____

Rate this recipe: Excellent ____ *Good* ____ *Average* ____

Additional Comments _____

_____

_____

Name of Recipe

_____

Name of Cookbook   *Page number*

_____

Date first prepared _____

Rate this recipe: Excellent ____ *Good* ____ *Average* ____

Additional Comments _____

_____

_____

▬▬▬▬▬▬▬▬▬▬▬▬▬▬▬▬▬▬▬▬▬▬▬▬▬▬

Name of Recipe

_____

Name of Cookbook   *Page number*

_____

Date first prepared _____

Rate this recipe: Excellent ____ *Good* ____ *Average* ____

Additional Comments _____

_____

_____

Name of Recipe

Name of Cookbook   *Page number*

Date first prepared _____

Rate this recipe: Excellent ____ *Good* ____ *Average* ____

Additional Comments _____

_____

_____

Name of Recipe

Name of Cookbook   *Page number*

Date first prepared _____

Rate this recipe: Excellent ____ *Good* ____ *Average* ____

Additional Comments _____

_____

_____

16   Soups

Name of Recipe

_____

Name of Cookbook   *Page number*

_____

Date first prepared _____

Rate this recipe: Excellent ____ Good ____ Average____

Additional Comments _____

_____

_____

Name of Recipe

_____

Name of Cookbook   *Page number*

_____

Date first prepared _____

Rate this recipe: Excellent ____ Good ____ Average____

Additional Comments _____

_____

_____

Name of Recipe

_____

Name of Cookbook   *Page number*

_____

Date first prepared _____

Rate this recipe: *Excellent* ____ *Good* ____ *Average* ____

Additional Comments _____

_____

_____

Name of Recipe

_____

Name of Cookbook   *Page number*

_____

Date first prepared _____

Rate this recipe: *Excellent* ____ *Good* ____ *Average* ____

Additional Comments _____

_____

_____

Name of Recipe

_____

Name of Cookbook   *Page number*

_____

Date first prepared _____

Rate this recipe: Excellent ___ Good ___ Average___

Additional Comments _____

_____

_____

Name of Recipe

_____

Name of Cookbook   *Page number*

_____

Date first prepared _____

Rate this recipe: Excellent ___ Good ___ Average___

Additional Comments _____

_____

_____

Name of Recipe

Name of Cookbook   *Page number*

Date first prepared _____

Rate this recipe: Excellent ____ *Good* ____ *Average* ____

Additional Comments _____

═══════════════════════════════════════

Name of Recipe

Name of Cookbook   *Page number*

Date first prepared _____

Rate this recipe: Excellent ____ *Good* ____ *Average* ____

Additional Comments _____

Name of Recipe

_____

Name of Cookbook   *Page number*

_____

Date first prepared _____

Rate this recipe: Excellent ____ *Good* ____ *Average* ____

Additional Comments _____

_____

_____

_____

━━━

Name of Recipe

_____

Name of Cookbook   *Page number*

_____

Date first prepared _____

Rate this recipe: Excellent ____ *Good* ____ *Average* ____

Additional Comments _____

_____

_____

Name of Recipe

_____

Name of Cookbook　　　　　　　　*Page number*

_____

Date first prepared _____

Rate this recipe: Excellent ____ *Good* ____ *Average*____

Additional Comments _____

_____

_____

Name of Recipe

_____

Name of Cookbook　　　　　　　　*Page number*

_____

Date first prepared _____

Rate this recipe: Excellent ____ *Good* ____ *Average*____

Additional Comments _____

_____

_____

Name of Recipe

_____

Name of Cookbook   *Page number*

_____

Date first prepared _____

Rate this recipe: Excellent ____ *Good* ____ *Average* ____

Additional Comments _____

_____

_____

Name of Recipe

_____

Name of Cookbook   *Page number*

_____

Date first prepared _____

Rate this recipe: Excellent ____ *Good* ____ *Average* ____

Additional Comments _____

_____

_____

Salads

Name of Recipe

_____

Name of Cookbook   Page number

_____

Date first prepared _____

Rate this recipe: Excellent ____ Good ____ Average ____

Additional Comments _____

_____

_____

Name of Recipe

_____

Name of Cookbook   *Page number*

_____

Date first prepared _____

Rate this recipe: Excellent ____ *Good* ____ *Average* ____

Additional Comments _____

_____

_____

Name of Recipe

_____

Name of Cookbook   *Page number*

_____

Date first prepared _____

Rate this recipe: Excellent ____ *Good* ____ *Average* ____

Additional Comments _____

_____

_____

Name of Recipe

_____

Name of Cookbook   *Page number*

_____

Date first prepared _____

Rate this recipe: Excellent ____ *Good* ____ *Average* ____

Additional Comments _____

_____

_____

Name of Recipe

_____

Name of Cookbook   *Page number*

_____

Date first prepared _____

Rate this recipe: Excellent ____ *Good* ____ *Average* ____

Additional Comments _____

_____

_____

Name of Recipe

_____

Name of Cookbook   *Page number*

_____

Date first prepared _____

Rate this recipe: Excellent ____ *Good* ____ *Average* ____

Additional Comments _____

_____

_____

_____

Name of Recipe

_____

Name of Cookbook   *Page number*

_____

Date first prepared _____

Rate this recipe: Excellent ____ *Good* ____ *Average* ____

Additional Comments _____

_____

_____

Name of Recipe

_____

Name of Cookbook   *Page number*

_____

Date first prepared _____

Rate this recipe: *Excellent* ____ *Good* ____ *Average* ____

Additional Comments _____

_____

_____

Name of Recipe

_____

Name of Cookbook   *Page number*

_____

Date first prepared _____

Rate this recipe: *Excellent* ____ *Good* ____ *Average* ____

Additional Comments _____

_____

_____

Name of Recipe

_____

Name of Cookbook   Page number

_____

Date first prepared _____

Rate this recipe: Excellent ____ Good ____ Average____

Additional Comments _____

_____

_____

Name of Recipe

_____

Name of Cookbook   Page number

_____

Date first prepared _____

Rate this recipe: Excellent ____ Good ____ Average____

Additional Comments _____

_____

_____

Name of Recipe

_____

Name of Cookbook   *Page number*

_____

Date first prepared _____

Rate this recipe: *Excellent* ____ *Good* ____ *Average* ____

Additional Comments _____

_____

_____

Name of Recipe

_____

Name of Cookbook   *Page number*

_____

Date first prepared _____

Rate this recipe: *Excellent* ____ *Good* ____ *Average* ____

Additional Comments _____

_____

_____

Name of Recipe

_____

Name of Cookbook   *Page number*

_____

Date first prepared _____

Rate this recipe: Excellent ____ Good ____ Average____

Additional Comments _____

_____

_____

Name of Recipe

_____

Name of Cookbook   *Page number*

_____

Date first prepared _____

Rate this recipe: Excellent ____ Good ____ Average____

Additional Comments _____

_____

_____

Name of Recipe

_____

Name of Cookbook   *Page number*

_____

Date first prepared _____

Rate this recipe: *Excellent* ____ *Good* ____ *Average* ____

Additional Comments _____

_____

_____

━━

Name of Recipe

_____

Name of Cookbook   *Page number*

_____

Date first prepared _____

Rate this recipe: *Excellent* ____ *Good* ____ *Average* ____

Additional Comments _____

_____

_____

Name of Recipe

_____

Name of Cookbook   *Page number*

_____

Date first prepared _____

Rate this recipe: Excellent ____ *Good* ____ *Average* ____

Additional Comments _____

_____

_____

Name of Recipe

_____

Name of Cookbook   *Page number*

_____

Date first prepared _____

Rate this recipe: Excellent ____ *Good* ____ *Average* ____

Additional Comments _____

_____

_____

Vegetables/Side Dishes

Name of Recipe   *Main ingredient*

_____

Name of Cookbook   *Page number*

_____

Date first prepared _____

Rate this recipe: *Excellent* ____ *Good* ____ *Average* ____

Additional Comments _____

_____

_____

Name of Recipe   Main ingredient

_____

Name of Cookbook   Page number

_____

Date first prepared _____

Rate this recipe: Excellent ____ Good ____ Average____

Additional Comments _____

_____

_____

Name of Recipe   Main ingredient

_____

Name of Cookbook   Page number

_____

Date first prepared _____

Rate this recipe: Excellent ____ Good ____ Average____

Additional Comments _____

_____

_____

Name of Recipe   Main ingredient

_____

Name of Cookbook   Page number

_____

Date first prepared _____

Rate this recipe: Excellent ____ Good ____ Average____

Additional Comments _____

_____

_____

═══

Name of Recipe   Main ingredient

_____

Name of Cookbook   Page number

_____

Date first prepared _____

Rate this recipe: Excellent ____ Good ____ Average____

Additional Comments _____

_____

_____

Name of Recipe   *Main ingredient*

_____

Name of Cookbook   *Page number*

_____

Date first prepared _____

Rate this recipe: Excellent ____ *Good* ____ *Average* ____

Additional Comments _____

_____

_____

Name of Recipe   *Main ingredient*

_____

Name of Cookbook   *Page number*

_____

Date first prepared _____

Rate this recipe: Excellent ____ *Good* ____ *Average* ____

Additional Comments _____

_____

_____

Name of Recipe   Main ingredient

_____

Name of Cookbook   Page number

_____

Date first prepared _____

Rate this recipe: Excellent ____ Good ____ Average ____

Additional Comments _____

_____

_____

Name of Recipe   Main ingredient

_____

Name of Cookbook   Page number

_____

Date first prepared _____

Rate this recipe: Excellent ____ Good ____ Average ____

Additional Comments _____

_____

_____

Name of Recipe   *Main ingredient*

_____

Name of Cookbook   *Page number*

_____

Date first prepared _____

Rate this recipe: *Excellent* ___ *Good* ___ *Average* ___

Additional Comments _____

_____

_____

Name of Recipe   *Main ingredient*

_____

Name of Cookbook   *Page number*

_____

Date first prepared _____

Rate this recipe: *Excellent* ___ *Good* ___ *Average* ___

Additional Comments _____

_____

_____

Name of Recipe   Main ingredient

_____

Name of Cookbook   Page number

_____

Date first prepared _____

Rate this recipe: Excellent ___ Good ___ Average___

Additional Comments _____

_____

_____

Name of Recipe   Main ingredient

_____

Name of Cookbook   Page number

_____

Date first prepared _____

Rate this recipe: Excellent ___ Good ___ Average___

Additional Comments _____

_____

_____

Name of Recipe   *Main ingredient*

_____

Name of Cookbook   *Page number*

_____

Date first prepared _____

Rate this recipe: Excellent ___ *Good* ___ *Average* ___

Additional Comments _____

_____

_____

━━━━━━━━━━━━━━━━━━━━━━━━━━━━━━━━━━━━━━

Name of Recipe   *Main ingredient*

_____

Name of Cookbook   *Page number*

_____

Date first prepared _____

Rate this recipe: Excellent ___ *Good* ___ *Average* ___

Additional Comments _____

_____

_____

Name of Recipe   Main ingredient

_____

Name of Cookbook   Page number

_____

Date first prepared _____

Rate this recipe: Excellent ____ Good ____ Average____

Additional Comments _____

_____

_____

Name of Recipe   Main ingredient

_____

Name of Cookbook   Page number

_____

Date first prepared _____

Rate this recipe: Excellent ____ Good ____ Average____

Additional Comments _____

_____

_____

Name of Recipe   *Main ingredient*

_____

Name of Cookbook   *Page number*

_____

Date first prepared _____

Rate this recipe: Excellent ____ Good ____ Average____

Additional Comments _____

_____

_____

Name of Recipe   *Main ingredient*

_____

Name of Cookbook   *Page number*

_____

Date first prepared _____

Rate this recipe: Excellent ____ Good ____ Average____

Additional Comments _____

_____

_____

Name of Recipe   *Main ingredient*

_____

Name of Cookbook   *Page number*

_____

Date first prepared _____

Rate this recipe: *Excellent* ____ *Good* ____ *Average* ____

Additional Comments _____

_____

_____

Name of Recipe   *Main ingredient*

_____

Name of Cookbook   *Page number*

_____

Date first prepared _____

Rate this recipe: *Excellent* ____ *Good* ____ *Average* ____

Additional Comments _____

_____

_____

Name of Recipe   Main ingredient

_____

Name of Cookbook   Page number

_____

Date first prepared _____

Rate this recipe: Excellent ____ Good ____ Average____

Additional Comments _____

_____

_____

Name of Recipe   Main ingredient

_____

Name of Cookbook   Page number

_____

Date first prepared _____

Rate this recipe: Excellent ____ Good ____ Average____

Additional Comments _____

_____

_____

Name of Recipe   Main ingredient

_____

Name of Cookbook   Page number

_____

Date first prepared _____

Rate this recipe: Excellent ____ Good ____ Average ____

Additional Comments _____

_____

_____

Name of Recipe   Main ingredient

_____

Name of Cookbook   Page number

_____

Date first prepared _____

Rate this recipe: Excellent ____ Good ____ Average ____

Additional Comments _____

_____

_____

Name of Recipe   Main ingredient

_____

Name of Cookbook   Page number

_____

Date first prepared _____

Rate this recipe: Excellent ____ Good ____ Average____

Additional Comments _____

_____

_____

Name of Recipe   Main ingredient

_____

Name of Cookbook   Page number

_____

Date first prepared _____

Rate this recipe: Excellent ____ Good ____ Average____

Additional Comments _____

_____

_____

Vegetables/Side Dishes 47

Name of Recipe   Main ingredient
_____

Name of Cookbook   Page number
_____

Date first prepared _____

Rate this recipe: Excellent ___ Good ___ Average___

Additional Comments _____

_____

_____

━━

Name of Recipe   Main ingredient
_____

Name of Cookbook   Page number
_____

Date first prepared _____

Rate this recipe: Excellent ___ Good ___ Average___

Additional Comments _____

_____

_____

Name of Recipe   Main ingredient

_____

Name of Cookbook   Page number

_____

Date first prepared _____

Rate this recipe: Excellent ____ Good ____ Average____

Additional Comments _____

_____

_____

Name of Recipe   Main ingredient

_____

Name of Cookbook   Page number

_____

Date first prepared _____

Rate this recipe: Excellent ____ Good ____ Average____

Additional Comments _____

_____

_____

Name of Recipe   Main ingredient

_____

Name of Cookbook   Page number

_____

Date first prepared _____

Rate this recipe: Excellent ____ Good ____ Average____

Additional Comments _____

_____

_____

Name of Recipe   Main ingredient

_____

Name of Cookbook   Page number

_____

Date first prepared _____

Rate this recipe: Excellent ____ Good ____ Average____

Additional Comments _____

_____

_____

Name of Recipe   *Main ingredient*

_____

Name of Cookbook   *Page number*

_____

Date first prepared _____

Rate this recipe: Excellent ___ *Good* ___ *Average*___

Additional Comments _____

_____

_____

Name of Recipe   *Main ingredient*

_____

Name of Cookbook   *Page number*

_____

Date first prepared _____

Rate this recipe: Excellent ___ *Good* ___ *Average*___

Additional Comments _____

_____

_____

Name of Recipe   *Main ingredient*

_____

Name of Cookbook   *Page number*

_____

Date first prepared _____

Rate this recipe: Excellent ____ *Good* ____ *Average* ____

Additional Comments _____

_____

_____

_____

Name of Recipe   *Main ingredient*

_____

Name of Cookbook   *Page number*

_____

Date first prepared _____

Rate this recipe: Excellent ____ *Good* ____ *Average* ____

Additional Comments _____

_____

_____

Name of Recipe   Main ingredient

_____

Name of Cookbook   Page number

_____

Date first prepared _____

Rate this recipe: Excellent ____ Good ____ Average____

Additional Comments _____

_____

_____

Name of Recipe   Main ingredient

_____

Name of Cookbook   Page number

_____

Date first prepared _____

Rate this recipe: Excellent ____ Good ____ Average____

Additional Comments _____

_____

_____

Name of Recipe   Main ingredient

_____

Name of Cookbook   Page number

_____

Date first prepared _____

Rate this recipe: Excellent ____ Good ____ Average____

Additional Comments _____

_____

_____

Name of Recipe   Main ingredient

_____

Name of Cookbook   Page number

_____

Date first prepared _____

Rate this recipe: Excellent ____ Good ____ Average____

Additional Comments _____

_____

_____

Name of Recipe   *Main ingredient*

_____

Name of Cookbook   *Page number*

_____

Date first prepared _____

Rate this recipe: Excellent ____ *Good* ____ *Average* ____

Additional Comments _____

_____

_____

_____

Name of Recipe   *Main ingredient*

_____

Name of Cookbook   *Page number*

_____

Date first prepared _____

Rate this recipe: Excellent ____ *Good* ____ *Average* ____

Additional Comments _____

_____

_____

Name of Recipe   Main ingredient

_____

Name of Cookbook   Page number

_____

Date first prepared _____

Rate this recipe: Excellent ____ Good ____ Average ____

Additional Comments _____

_____

_____

Name of Recipe   Main ingredient

_____

Name of Cookbook   Page number

_____

Date first prepared _____

Rate this recipe: Excellent ____ Good ____ Average ____

Additional Comments _____

_____

_____

Name of Recipe   Main ingredient

_____

Name of Cookbook   Page number

_____

Date first prepared _____

Rate this recipe: Excellent ____ Good ____ Average____

Additional Comments _____

_____

_____

Name of Recipe   Main ingredient

_____

Name of Cookbook   Page number

_____

Date first prepared _____

Rate this recipe: Excellent ____ Good ____ Average____

Additional Comments _____

_____

_____

Name of Recipe   Main ingredient

_____

Name of Cookbook   Page number

_____

Date first prepared _____

Rate this recipe: Excellent ____ Good ____ Average____

Additional Comments _____

_____

_____

═══

Name of Recipe   Main ingredient

_____

Name of Cookbook   Page number

_____

Date first prepared _____

Rate this recipe: Excellent ____ Good ____ Average____

Additional Comments _____

_____

_____

Name of Recipe   *Main ingredient*

_____

Name of Cookbook   *Page number*

_____

Date first prepared _____

Rate this recipe: Excellent ____ *Good* ____ *Average* ____

Additional Comments _____

_____

_____

Name of Recipe   *Main ingredient*

_____

Name of Cookbook   *Page number*

_____

Date first prepared _____

Rate this recipe: Excellent ____ *Good* ____ *Average* ____

Additional Comments _____

_____

_____

Pasta

Name of Recipe

_____

Name of Cookbook   *Page number*

_____

Date first prepared _____

Rate this recipe: Excellent ____ *Good* ____ *Average* ____

Additional Comments _____

_____

_____

Name of Recipe

_____

Name of Cookbook   *Page number*

_____

Date first prepared _____

Rate this recipe: Excellent ___ *Good* ___ *Average* ___

Additional Comments _____

_____

_____

_____

Name of Recipe

_____

Name of Cookbook   *Page number*

_____

Date first prepared _____

Rate this recipe: Excellent ___ *Good* ___ *Average* ___

Additional Comments _____

_____

_____

Name of Recipe

_____

Name of Cookbook   *Page number*

_____

Date first prepared _____

Rate this recipe: *Excellent* ____ *Good* ____ *Average* ____

Additional Comments _____

_____

_____

━━

Name of Recipe

_____

Name of Cookbook   *Page number*

_____

Date first prepared _____

Rate this recipe: *Excellent* ____ *Good* ____ *Average* ____

Additional Comments _____

_____

_____

Name of Recipe

_____

Name of Cookbook   *Page number*

_____

Date first prepared _____

Rate this recipe: Excellent ____ *Good* ____ *Average* ____

Additional Comments _____

_____

_____

_____

═══

Name of Recipe

_____

Name of Cookbook   *Page number*

_____

Date first prepared _____

Rate this recipe: Excellent ____ *Good* ____ *Average* ____

Additional Comments _____

_____

_____

Name of Recipe

_____

Name of Cookbook   *Page number*

_____

Date first prepared _____

Rate this recipe: *Excellent* ____ *Good* ____ *Average* ____

Additional Comments _____

_____

_____

Name of Recipe

_____

Name of Cookbook   *Page number*

_____

Date first prepared _____

Rate this recipe: *Excellent* ____ *Good* ____ *Average* ____

Additional Comments _____

_____

_____

Name of Recipe

_____

Name of Cookbook   *Page number*

_____

Date first prepared _____

Rate this recipe: Excellent ____ *Good* ____ *Average* ____

Additional Comments _____

_____

_____

Name of Recipe

_____

Name of Cookbook   *Page number*

_____

Date first prepared _____

Rate this recipe: Excellent ____ *Good* ____ *Average* ____

Additional Comments _____

_____

_____

Name of Recipe

_____

Name of Cookbook   *Page number*

_____

Date first prepared _____

Rate this recipe: Excellent ___ *Good* ___ *Average* ___

Additional Comments _____

_____

_____

Name of Recipe

_____

Name of Cookbook   *Page number*

_____

Date first prepared _____

Rate this recipe: Excellent ___ *Good* ___ *Average* ___

Additional Comments _____

_____

_____

Name of Recipe

_____

Name of Cookbook   *Page number*

_____

Date first prepared _____

Rate this recipe: *Excellent* ____ *Good* ____ *Average* ____

Additional Comments _____

_____

_____

Name of Recipe

_____

Name of Cookbook   *Page number*

_____

Date first prepared _____

Rate this recipe: *Excellent* ____ *Good* ____ *Average* ____

Additional Comments _____

_____

_____

Name of Recipe

_____

Name of Cookbook   *Page number*

_____

Date first prepared _____

Rate this recipe: Excellent ___ *Good* ___ *Average* ___

Additional Comments _____

_____

_____

Name of Recipe

_____

Name of Cookbook   *Page number*

_____

Date first prepared _____

Rate this recipe: Excellent ___ *Good* ___ *Average* ___

Additional Comments _____

_____

_____

Name of Recipe

_____

Name of Cookbook   *Page number*

_____

Date first prepared _____

Rate this recipe: Excellent ___ *Good* ___ *Average* ___

Additional Comments _____

_____

_____

_____

━━

Name of Recipe   *Main ingredient*

_____

Name of Cookbook   *Page number*

_____

Date first prepared _____

Rate this recipe: Excellent ___ *Good* ___ *Average* ___

Additional Comments _____

_____

_____

Casseroles

Name of Recipe   Main ingredient

_____

Name of Cookbook   Page number

_____

Date first prepared _____

Rate this recipe: Excellent ____ Good ____ Average ____

Additional Comments _____

_____

_____

Name of Recipe   Main ingredient

_____

Name of Cookbook   Page number

_____

Date first prepared _____

Rate this recipe: Excellent ____ Good ____ Average____

Additional Comments _____

_____

_____

Name of Recipe   Main ingredient

_____

Name of Cookbook   Page number

_____

Date first prepared _____

Rate this recipe: Excellent ____ Good ____ Average____

Additional Comments _____

_____

_____

Name of Recipe   Main ingredient

_____

Name of Cookbook   Page number

_____

Date first prepared _____

Rate this recipe: Excellent ____ Good ____ Average____

Additional Comments _____

_____

_____

══

Name of Recipe   Main ingredient

_____

Name of Cookbook   Page number

_____

Date first prepared _____

Rate this recipe: Excellent ____ Good ____ Average____

Additional Comments _____

_____

_____

Name of Recipe   *Main ingredient*

_____

Name of Cookbook   *Page number*

_____

Date first prepared _____

Rate this recipe: *Excellent* ___ *Good* ___ *Average* ___

Additional Comments _____

_____

_____

_____

Name of Recipe   *Main ingredient*

_____

Name of Cookbook   *Page number*

_____

Date first prepared _____

Rate this recipe: *Excellent* ___ *Good* ___ *Average* ___

Additional Comments _____

_____

_____

Name of Recipe   Main ingredient

_____

Name of Cookbook   Page number

_____

Date first prepared _____

Rate this recipe: Excellent ____ Good ____ Average____

Additional Comments _____

_____

_____

Name of Recipe   Main ingredient

_____

Name of Cookbook   Page number

_____

Date first prepared _____

Rate this recipe: Excellent ____ Good ____ Average____

Additional Comments _____

_____

_____

Name of Recipe   *Main ingredient*

_____

Name of Cookbook   *Page number*

_____

Date first prepared _____

Rate this recipe: Excellent ____ *Good* ____ *Average* ____

Additional Comments _____

_____

_____

_____

Name of Recipe   *Main ingredient*

_____

Name of Cookbook   *Page number*

_____

Date first prepared _____

Rate this recipe: Excellent ____ *Good* ____ *Average* ____

Additional Comments _____

_____

_____

Name of Recipe   Main ingredient

_____

Name of Cookbook   Page number

_____

Date first prepared _____

Rate this recipe: Excellent ____ Good ____ Average____

Additional Comments _____

_____

_____

Name of Recipe   Main ingredient

_____

Name of Cookbook   Page number

_____

Date first prepared _____

Rate this recipe: Excellent ____ Good ____ Average____

Additional Comments _____

_____

_____

Name of Recipe   Main ingredient

_____

Name of Cookbook   Page number

_____

Date first prepared _____

Rate this recipe: Excellent ___ Good ___ Average___

Additional Comments _____

_____

_____

Name of Recipe   Main ingredient

_____

Name of Cookbook   Page number

_____

Date first prepared _____

Rate this recipe: Excellent ___ Good ___ Average___

Additional Comments _____

_____

_____

Name of Recipe   Main ingredient

_____

Name of Cookbook   Page number

_____

Date first prepared _____

Rate this recipe: Excellent ___ Good ___ Average___

Additional Comments _____

_____

_____

Name of Recipe   Main ingredient

_____

Name of Cookbook   Page number

_____

Date first prepared _____

Rate this recipe: Excellent ___ Good ___ Average___

Additional Comments _____

_____

_____

Name of Recipe   Main ingredient

_____

Name of Cookbook   Page number

_____

Date first prepared _____

Rate this recipe: Excellent ____ Good ____ Average____

Additional Comments _____

_____

_____

Name of Recipe   Main ingredient

_____

Name of Cookbook   Page number

_____

Date first prepared _____

Rate this recipe: Excellent ____ Good ____ Average____

Additional Comments _____

_____

_____

Name of Recipe   Main ingredient

_____

Name of Cookbook   Page number

_____

Date first prepared _____

Rate this recipe: Excellent ____ Good ____ Average ____

Additional Comments _____

_____

_____

Name of Recipe   Main ingredient

_____

Name of Cookbook   Page number

_____

Date first prepared _____

Rate this recipe: Excellent ____ Good ____ Average ____

Additional Comments _____

_____

_____

Name of Recipe   Main ingredient

_____

Name of Cookbook   Page number

_____

Date first prepared _____

Rate this recipe: Excellent ____ Good ____ Average____

Additional Comments _____

_____

_____

Name of Recipe   Main ingredient

_____

Name of Cookbook   Page number

_____

Date first prepared _____

Rate this recipe: Excellent ____ Good ____ Average____

Additional Comments _____

_____

_____

Name of Recipe   *Main ingredient*

_____

Name of Cookbook   *Page number*

_____

Date first prepared _____

Rate this recipe: *Excellent* ____ *Good* ____ *Average* ____

Additional Comments _____

_____

_____

Name of Recipe   *Main ingredient*

_____

Name of Cookbook   *Page number*

_____

Date first prepared _____

Rate this recipe: *Excellent* ____ *Good* ____ *Average* ____

Additional Comments _____

_____

_____

Name of Recipe   Main ingredient

_____

Name of Cookbook   Page number

_____

Date first prepared _____

Rate this recipe: Excellent ____ Good ____ Average____

Additional Comments _____

_____

_____

═══

Name of Recipe   Main ingredient

_____

Name of Cookbook   Page number

_____

Date first prepared _____

Rate this recipe: Excellent ____ Good ____ Average____

Additional Comments _____

_____

_____

Name of Recipe   *Main ingredient*

_____

Name of Cookbook   *Page number*

_____

Date first prepared _____

Rate this recipe: *Excellent* ____ *Good* ____ *Average*____

Additional Comments _____

_____

_____

Name of Recipe   *Main ingredient*

_____

Name of Cookbook   *Page number*

_____

Date first prepared _____

Rate this recipe: *Excellent* ____ *Good* ____ *Average*____

Additional Comments _____

_____

_____

Name of Recipe   *Main ingredient*

_____

Name of Cookbook   *Page number*

_____

Date first prepared _____

Rate this recipe: Excellent ____ *Good* ____ *Average* ____

Additional Comments _____

_____

_____

Name of Recipe   *Main ingredient*

_____

Name of Cookbook   *Page number*

_____

Date first prepared _____

Rate this recipe: Excellent ____ *Good* ____ *Average* ____

Additional Comments _____

_____

_____

Name of Recipe   *Main ingredient*

_____

Name of Cookbook   *Page number*

_____

Date first prepared _____

Rate this recipe: *Excellent* ____ *Good* ____ *Average* ____

Additional Comments _____

_____

_____

Name of Recipe   *Main ingredient*

_____

Name of Cookbook   *Page number*

_____

Date first prepared _____

Rate this recipe: *Excellent* ____ *Good* ____ *Average* ____

Additional Comments _____

_____

_____

Name of Recipe   *Main ingredient*

_____

Name of Cookbook   *Page number*

_____

Date first prepared _____

Rate this recipe: *Excellent* ____ *Good* ____ *Average* ____

Additional Comments _____

_____

_____

_____

Name of Recipe   *Main ingredient*

_____

Name of Cookbook   *Page number*

_____

Date first prepared _____

Rate this recipe: *Excellent* ____ *Good* ____ *Average* ____

Additional Comments _____

_____

_____

Name of Recipe   Main ingredient

_____

Name of Cookbook   Page number

_____

Date first prepared _____

Rate this recipe: Excellent ____ Good ____ Average ____

Additional Comments _____

_____

_____

═══

Name of Recipe   Main ingredient

_____

Name of Cookbook   Page number

_____

Date first prepared _____

Rate this recipe: Excellent ____ Good ____ Average ____

Additional Comments _____

_____

_____

Name of Recipe   Main ingredient

_____

Name of Cookbook   Page number

_____

Date first prepared _____

Rate this recipe: Excellent ____ Good ____ Average____

Additional Comments _____

_____

_____

Name of Recipe   Main ingredient

_____

Name of Cookbook   Page number

_____

Date first prepared _____

Rate this recipe: Excellent ____ Good ____ Average____

Additional Comments _____

_____

_____

Beef

Name of Recipe

_____

Name of Cookbook   *Page number*

_____

Date first prepared _____

Rate this recipe: Excellent ____ *Good* ____ *Average* ____

Additional Comments _____

_____

_____

Name of Recipe

_____

Name of Cookbook   *Page number*

_____

Date first prepared _____

Rate this recipe: Excellent ___ *Good* ___ *Average* ___

Additional Comments _____

_____

_____

_____

Name of Recipe

_____

Name of Cookbook   *Page number*

_____

Date first prepared _____

Rate this recipe: Excellent ___ *Good* ___ *Average* ___

Additional Comments _____

_____

_____

Name of Recipe

_____

Name of Cookbook   *Page number*

_____

Date first prepared _____

Rate this recipe: *Excellent* ____ *Good* ____ *Average* ____

Additional Comments _____

_____

_____

═══

Name of Recipe

_____

Name of Cookbook   *Page number*

_____

Date first prepared _____

Rate this recipe: *Excellent* ____ *Good* ____ *Average* ____

Additional Comments _____

_____

_____

Name of Recipe

_____

Name of Cookbook   Page number

_____

Date first prepared _____

Rate this recipe: Excellent ____ Good ____ Average____

Additional Comments _____

_____

_____

_____

Name of Recipe

_____

Name of Cookbook   Page number

_____

Date first prepared _____

Rate this recipe: Excellent ____ Good ____ Average____

Additional Comments _____

_____

_____

Name of Recipe

Name of Cookbook   *Page number*

Date first prepared _____

Rate this recipe: *Excellent* ___ *Good* ___ *Average* ___

Additional Comments _____

_____

_____

Name of Recipe

Name of Cookbook   *Page number*

Date first prepared _____

Rate this recipe: *Excellent* ___ *Good* ___ *Average* ___

Additional Comments _____

_____

_____

Name of Recipe

_____

Name of Cookbook   Page number

_____

Date first prepared _____

Rate this recipe: Excellent ___ Good ___ Average___

Additional Comments _____

_____

_____

Name of Recipe

_____

Name of Cookbook   Page number

_____

Date first prepared _____

Rate this recipe: Excellent ___ Good ___ Average___

Additional Comments _____

_____

_____

Name of Recipe

_____

Name of Cookbook   *Page number*

_____

Date first prepared _____

Rate this recipe: *Excellent* ___ *Good* ___ *Average* ___

Additional Comments _____

_____

_____

Name of Recipe

_____

Name of Cookbook   *Page number*

_____

Date first prepared _____

Rate this recipe: *Excellent* ___ *Good* ___ *Average* ___

Additional Comments _____

_____

_____

Name of Recipe

_____

Name of Cookbook   *Page number*

_____

Date first prepared _____

Rate this recipe: Excellent ___ *Good* ___ *Average* ___

Additional Comments _____

_____

_____

Name of Recipe

_____

Name of Cookbook   *Page number*

_____

Date first prepared _____

Rate this recipe: Excellent ___ *Good* ___ *Average* ___

Additional Comments _____

_____

_____

Name of Recipe

_____

Name of Cookbook   *Page number*

_____

Date first prepared _____

Rate this recipe: *Excellent* ____ *Good* ____ *Average* ____

Additional Comments _____

_____

_____

_____

Name of Recipe

_____

Name of Cookbook   *Page number*

_____

Date first prepared _____

Rate this recipe: *Excellent* ____ *Good* ____ *Average* ____

Additional Comments _____

_____

_____

Name of Recipe

_____

Name of Cookbook   Page number

_____

Date first prepared _____

Rate this recipe: Excellent ____ Good ____ Average____

Additional Comments _____

_____

_____

Name of Recipe

_____

Name of Cookbook   Page number

_____

Date first prepared _____

Rate this recipe: Excellent ____ Good ____ Average____

Additional Comments _____

_____

_____

Name of Recipe

_____

Name of Cookbook   *Page number*

_____

Date first prepared _____

Rate this recipe: *Excellent* ___ *Good* ___ *Average* ___

Additional Comments _____

_____

_____

═══

Name of Recipe

_____

Name of Cookbook   *Page number*

_____

Date first prepared _____

Rate this recipe: *Excellent* ___ *Good* ___ *Average* ___

Additional Comments _____

_____

_____

Name of Recipe

_____

Name of Cookbook   *Page number*

_____

Date first prepared _____

Rate this recipe: Excellent ___ Good ___ Average___

Additional Comments _____

_____

_____

Name of Recipe

_____

Name of Cookbook   *Page number*

_____

Date first prepared _____

Rate this recipe: Excellent ___ Good ___ Average___

Additional Comments _____

_____

_____

Name of Recipe

_____

Name of Cookbook   *Page number*

_____

Date first prepared _____

Rate this recipe: *Excellent* ____ *Good* ____ *Average* ____

Additional Comments _____

_____

_____

━━━

Name of Recipe

_____

Name of Cookbook   *Page number*

_____

Date first prepared _____

Rate this recipe: *Excellent* ____ *Good* ____ *Average* ____

Additional Comments _____

_____

_____

Name of Recipe

_____

Name of Cookbook   *Page number*

_____

Date first prepared _____

Rate this recipe: Excellent ____ *Good* ____ *Average* ____

Additional Comments _____

_____

_____

Name of Recipe

_____

Name of Cookbook   *Page number*

_____

Date first prepared _____

Rate this recipe: Excellent ____ *Good* ____ *Average* ____

Additional Comments _____

_____

_____

Name of Recipe

_____

Name of Cookbook   *Page number*

_____

Date first prepared _____

Rate this recipe: *Excellent* ____ *Good* ____ *Average* ____

Additional Comments _____

_____

_____

━━━━━━━━━━━━━━━━━━━━━━━━━━━━━━━━━━━━━━━

Name of Recipe

_____

Name of Cookbook   *Page number*

_____

Date first prepared _____

Rate this recipe: *Excellent* ____ *Good* ____ *Average* ____

Additional Comments _____

_____

_____

Name of Recipe

_____

Name of Cookbook   *Page number*

_____

Date first prepared _____

Rate this recipe: Excellent ___ *Good* ___ *Average* ___

Additional Comments _____

_____

_____

_____

Name of Recipe

_____

Name of Cookbook   *Page number*

_____

Date first prepared _____

Rate this recipe: Excellent ___ *Good* ___ *Average* ___

Additional Comments _____

_____

_____

Name of Recipe

_____

Name of Cookbook   *Page number*

_____

Date first prepared _____

Rate this recipe: Excellent ____ Good ____ Average____

Additional Comments _____

_____

_____

Name of Recipe

_____

Name of Cookbook   *Page number*

_____

Date first prepared _____

Rate this recipe: Excellent ____ Good ____ Average____

Additional Comments _____

_____

_____

Name of Recipe

_____

Name of Cookbook   *Page number*

_____

Date first prepared _____

Rate this recipe: Excellent ____ Good ____ Average____

Additional Comments _____

_____

_____

Name of Recipe   *Main ingredient*

_____

Name of Cookbook   *Page number*

_____

Date first prepared _____

Rate this recipe: Excellent ____ Good ____ Average____

Additional Comments _____

_____

_____

Name of Recipe

_____

Name of Cookbook   *Page number*

_____

Date first prepared _____

Rate this recipe: *Excellent* ____ *Good* ____ *Average* ____

Additional Comments _____

_____

_____

Name of Recipe   *Main ingredient*

_____

Name of Cookbook   *Page number*

_____

Date first prepared _____

Rate this recipe: *Excellent* ____ *Good* ____ *Average* ____

Additional Comments _____

_____

_____

Pork

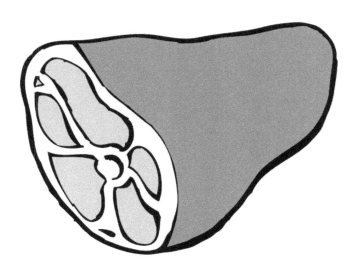

Name of Recipe

_____

Name of Cookbook   Page number

_____

Date first prepared _____

Rate this recipe: Excellent ____ Good ____ Average____

Additional Comments _____

_____

_____

Name of Recipe

_____

Name of Cookbook   *Page number*

_____

Date first prepared _____

Rate this recipe: *Excellent* ____ *Good* ____ *Average* ____

Additional Comments _____

_____

_____

_____

Name of Recipe

_____

Name of Cookbook   *Page number*

_____

Date first prepared _____

Rate this recipe: *Excellent* ____ *Good* ____ *Average* ____

Additional Comments _____

_____

_____

Name of Recipe

_____

Name of Cookbook   Page number

_____

Date first prepared _____

Rate this recipe: Excellent ____ Good ____ Average____

Additional Comments _____

_____

_____

Name of Recipe

_____

Name of Cookbook   Page number

_____

Date first prepared _____

Rate this recipe: Excellent ____ Good ____ Average____

Additional Comments _____

_____

_____

Name of Recipe

Name of Cookbook   *Page number*

Date first prepared _____

Rate this recipe: *Excellent* ___ *Good* ___ *Average*___

Additional Comments _____

_____

_____

Name of Recipe

Name of Cookbook   *Page number*

Date first prepared _____

Rate this recipe: *Excellent* ___ *Good* ___ *Average*___

Additional Comments _____

_____

_____

Name of Recipe

_____

Name of Cookbook   *Page number*

_____

Date first prepared _____

Rate this recipe: Excellent ____ Good ____ Average____

Additional Comments _____

_____

_____

Name of Recipe

_____

Name of Cookbook   *Page number*

_____

Date first prepared _____

Rate this recipe: Excellent ____ Good ____ Average____

Additional Comments _____

_____

_____

Name of Recipe

Name of Cookbook   *Page number*

Date first prepared _____

Rate this recipe: *Excellent* ____ *Good* ____ *Average* ____

Additional Comments _____

_____

_____

Name of Recipe

Name of Cookbook   *Page number*

Date first prepared _____

Rate this recipe: *Excellent* ____ *Good* ____ *Average* ____

Additional Comments _____

_____

_____

Name of Recipe

_____

Name of Cookbook   *Page number*

_____

Date first prepared _____

Rate this recipe: Excellent ___ *Good* ___ *Average*___

Additional Comments _____

_____

_____

Name of Recipe

_____

Name of Cookbook   *Page number*

_____

Date first prepared _____

Rate this recipe: Excellent ___ *Good* ___ *Average*___

Additional Comments _____

_____

_____

Name of Recipe

Name of Cookbook   *Page number*

Date first prepared _____

Rate this recipe: Excellent ___ *Good* ___ *Average* ___

Additional Comments _____

_____

_____

Name of Recipe

Name of Cookbook   *Page number*

Date first prepared _____

Rate this recipe: Excellent ___ *Good* ___ *Average* ___

Additional Comments _____

_____

_____

Name of Recipe

_____

Name of Cookbook   *Page number*

_____

Date first prepared _____

Rate this recipe: Excellent ____ *Good* ____ *Average* ____

Additional Comments _____

_____

_____

Name of Recipe

_____

Name of Cookbook   *Page number*

_____

Date first prepared _____

Rate this recipe: Excellent ____ *Good* ____ *Average* ____

Additional Comments _____

_____

_____

Name of Recipe

_____

Name of Cookbook   *Page number*

_____

Date first prepared _____

Rate this recipe: *Excellent* ____ *Good* ____ *Average* ____

Additional Comments _____

_____

_____

Name of Recipe

_____

Name of Cookbook   *Page number*

_____

Date first prepared _____

Rate this recipe: *Excellent* ____ *Good* ____ *Average* ____

Additional Comments _____

_____

_____

Name of Recipe

_____

Name of Cookbook   *Page number*

_____

Date first prepared _____

Rate this recipe: Excellent ___ *Good* ___ *Average* ___

Additional Comments _____

_____

_____

Name of Recipe

_____

Name of Cookbook   *Page number*

_____

Date first prepared _____

Rate this recipe: Excellent ___ *Good* ___ *Average* ___

Additional Comments _____

_____

_____

Name of Recipe

_____

Name of Cookbook   *Page number*

_____

Date first prepared _____

Rate this recipe: *Excellent* ____ *Good* ____ *Average* ____

Additional Comments _____

_____

_____

Name of Recipe

_____

Name of Cookbook   *Page number*

_____

Date first prepared _____

Rate this recipe: *Excellent* ____ *Good* ____ *Average* ____

Additional Comments _____

_____

_____

Name of Recipe

_____

Name of Cookbook   *Page number*

_____

Date first prepared _____

Rate this recipe: Excellent ____ *Good* ____ *Average* ____

Additional Comments _____

_____

_____

Name of Recipe

_____

Name of Cookbook   *Page number*

_____

Date first prepared _____

Rate this recipe: Excellent ____ *Good* ____ *Average* ____

Additional Comments _____

_____

_____

Name of Recipe

_____

Name of Cookbook   *Page number*

_____

Date first prepared _____

Rate this recipe: *Excellent* ____ *Good* ____ *Average* ____

Additional Comments _____

_____

_____

Name of Recipe

_____

Name of Cookbook   *Page number*

_____

Date first prepared _____

Rate this recipe: *Excellent* ____ *Good* ____ *Average* ____

Additional Comments _____

_____

_____

Name of Recipe

_____

Name of Cookbook   *Page number*

_____

Date first prepared _____

Rate this recipe: Excellent ___ *Good* ___ *Average* ___

Additional Comments _____

_____

_____

Name of Recipe

_____

Name of Cookbook   *Page number*

_____

Date first prepared _____

Rate this recipe: Excellent ___ *Good* ___ *Average* ___

Additional Comments _____

_____

_____

Name of Recipe

Name of Cookbook   *Page number*

Date first prepared _____

Rate this recipe: *Excellent* ___ *Good* ___ *Average* ___

Additional Comments _____

_____

_____

Name of Recipe

Name of Cookbook   *Page number*

Date first prepared _____

Rate this recipe: *Excellent* ___ *Good* ___ *Average* ___

Additional Comments _____

_____

_____

Name of Recipe

_____

Name of Cookbook   *Page number*

_____

Date first prepared _____

Rate this recipe: Excellent ____ Good ____ Average____

Additional Comments _____

_____

_____

Name of Recipe

_____

Name of Cookbook   *Page number*

_____

Date first prepared _____

Rate this recipe: Excellent ____ Good ____ Average____

Additional Comments _____

_____

_____

Name of Recipe

_____

Name of Cookbook   *Page number*

_____

Date first prepared _____

Rate this recipe: *Excellent* ____ *Good* ____ *Average* ____

Additional Comments _____

_____

_____

Name of Recipe

_____

Name of Cookbook   *Page number*

_____

Date first prepared _____

Rate this recipe: *Excellent* ____ *Good* ____ *Average* ____

Additional Comments _____

_____

_____

Name of Recipe

_____

Name of Cookbook   *Page number*

_____

Date first prepared _____

Rate this recipe: Excellent ____ *Good* ____ *Average*____

Additional Comments _____

_____

_____

Name of Recipe   *Main ingredient*

_____

Name of Cookbook   *Page number*

_____

Date first prepared _____

Rate this recipe: Excellent ____ *Good* ____ *Average*____

Additional Comments _____

_____

_____

Name of Recipe
_____

Name of Cookbook   *Page number*
_____

Date first prepared _____

Rate this recipe: *Excellent* ___ *Good* ___ *Average* ___

Additional Comments _____

_____

_____

═══

Name of Recipe   *Main ingredient*
_____

Name of Cookbook   *Page number*
_____

Date first prepared _____

Rate this recipe: *Excellent* ___ *Good* ___ *Average* ___

Additional Comments _____

_____

_____

Chicken

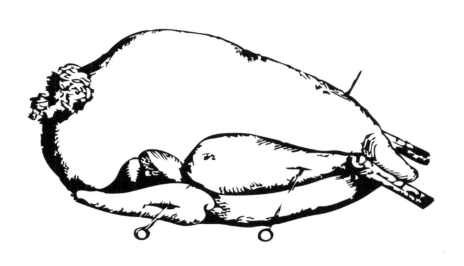

Name of Recipe

_____

Name of Cookbook   *Page number*

_____

Date first prepared _____

Rate this recipe: Excellent ____ *Good* ____ *Average* ____

Additional Comments _____

_____

_____

Name of Recipe

Name of Cookbook   *Page number*

Date first prepared _____

Rate this recipe: Excellent ____ *Good* ____ *Average* ____

Additional Comments _____

Name of Recipe

Name of Cookbook   *Page number*

Date first prepared _____

Rate this recipe: Excellent ____ *Good* ____ *Average* ____

Additional Comments _____

Name of Recipe

_____

Name of Cookbook   *Page number*

_____

Date first prepared _____

Rate this recipe: Excellent ____ Good ____ Average____

Additional Comments _____

_____

_____

Name of Recipe

_____

Name of Cookbook   *Page number*

_____

Date first prepared _____

Rate this recipe: Excellent ____ Good ____ Average____

Additional Comments _____

_____

_____

Name of Recipe

_____

Name of Cookbook   *Page number*

_____

Date first prepared _____

Rate this recipe: Excellent ____ *Good* ____ *Average* ____

Additional Comments _____

_____

_____

Name of Recipe

_____

Name of Cookbook   *Page number*

_____

Date first prepared _____

Rate this recipe: Excellent ____ *Good* ____ *Average* ____

Additional Comments _____

_____

_____

Name of Recipe

_____

Name of Cookbook   *Page number*

_____

Date first prepared _____

Rate this recipe: Excellent ____ *Good* ____ *Average*____

Additional Comments _____

_____

_____

Name of Recipe

_____

Name of Cookbook   *Page number*

_____

Date first prepared _____

Rate this recipe: Excellent ____ *Good* ____ *Average*____

Additional Comments _____

_____

_____

Name of Recipe

_____

Name of Cookbook   Page number

_____

Date first prepared _____

Rate this recipe: Excellent ____ Good ____ Average ____

Additional Comments _____

_____

_____

Name of Recipe

_____

Name of Cookbook   Page number

_____

Date first prepared _____

Rate this recipe: Excellent ____ Good ____ Average ____

Additional Comments _____

_____

_____

Name of Recipe

_____

Name of Cookbook   *Page number*

_____

Date first prepared _____

Rate this recipe: Excellent ____ *Good* ____ *Average* ____

Additional Comments _____

_____

_____

_____

Name of Recipe

_____

Name of Cookbook   *Page number*

_____

Date first prepared _____

Rate this recipe: Excellent ____ *Good* ____ *Average* ____

Additional Comments _____

_____

_____

Name of Recipe

_____

Name of Cookbook   *Page number*

_____

Date first prepared _____

Rate this recipe: *Excellent* ___ *Good* ___ *Average* ___

Additional Comments _____

_____

_____

Name of Recipe

_____

Name of Cookbook   *Page number*

_____

Date first prepared _____

Rate this recipe: *Excellent* ___ *Good* ___ *Average* ___

Additional Comments _____

_____

_____

Name of Recipe

_____

Name of Cookbook   Page number

_____

Date first prepared _____

Rate this recipe: Excellent ____ Good ____ Average____

Additional Comments _____

_____

_____

━━━

Name of Recipe

_____

Name of Cookbook   Page number

_____

Date first prepared _____

Rate this recipe: Excellent ____ Good ____ Average____

Additional Comments _____

_____

_____

Name of Recipe

_____

Name of Cookbook   Page number

_____

Date first prepared _____

Rate this recipe: Excellent ____ Good ____ Average____

Additional Comments _____

_____

_____

Name of Recipe

_____

Name of Cookbook   Page number

_____

Date first prepared _____

Rate this recipe: Excellent ____ Good ____ Average____

Additional Comments _____

_____

_____

Name of Recipe

_____

Name of Cookbook   *Page number*

_____

Date first prepared _____

Rate this recipe: Excellent ____ *Good* ____ *Average* ____

Additional Comments _____

_____

_____

Name of Recipe

_____

Name of Cookbook   *Page number*

_____

Date first prepared _____

Rate this recipe: Excellent ____ *Good* ____ *Average* ____

Additional Comments _____

_____

_____

Name of Recipe

_____

Name of Cookbook *Page number*

_____

Date first prepared _____

Rate this recipe: *Excellent* ___ *Good* ___ *Average* ___

Additional Comments _____

_____

_____

Name of Recipe

_____

Name of Cookbook *Page number*

_____

Date first prepared _____

Rate this recipe: *Excellent* ___ *Good* ___ *Average* ___

Additional Comments _____

_____

_____

Name of Recipe

_____

Name of Cookbook   *Page number*

_____

Date first prepared _____

Rate this recipe: Excellent ____ *Good* ____ *Average* ____

Additional Comments _____

_____

_____

Name of Recipe

_____

Name of Cookbook   *Page number*

_____

Date first prepared _____

Rate this recipe: Excellent ____ *Good* ____ *Average* ____

Additional Comments _____

_____

_____

Name of Recipe

_____

Name of Cookbook   Page number

_____

Date first prepared _____

Rate this recipe: Excellent ___ Good ___ Average___

Additional Comments _____

_____

_____

═══

Name of Recipe

_____

Name of Cookbook   Page number

_____

Date first prepared _____

Rate this recipe: Excellent ___ Good ___ Average___

Additional Comments _____

_____

_____

Name of Recipe

_____

Name of Cookbook   *Page number*

_____

Date first prepared _____

Rate this recipe: *Excellent* ___ *Good* ___ *Average* ___

Additional Comments _____

_____

_____

Name of Recipe

_____

Name of Cookbook   *Page number*

_____

Date first prepared _____

Rate this recipe: *Excellent* ___ *Good* ___ *Average* ___

Additional Comments _____

_____

_____

Name of Recipe

_____

Name of Cookbook   *Page number*

_____

Date first prepared _____

Rate this recipe: Excellent ___ *Good* ___ *Average* ___

Additional Comments _____

_____

_____

_____

Name of Recipe

_____

Name of Cookbook   *Page number*

_____

Date first prepared _____

Rate this recipe: Excellent ___ *Good* ___ *Average* ___

Additional Comments _____

_____

_____

Name of Recipe

_____

Name of Cookbook   *Page number*

_____

Date first prepared _____

Rate this recipe: Excellent ____ *Good* ____ *Average* ____

Additional Comments _____

_____

_____

Name of Recipe

_____

Name of Cookbook   *Page number*

_____

Date first prepared _____

Rate this recipe: Excellent ____ *Good* ____ *Average* ____

Additional Comments _____

_____

_____

Name of Recipe

_____

Name of Cookbook   *Page number*

_____

Date first prepared _____

Rate this recipe: *Excellent* ___ *Good* ___ *Average* ___

Additional Comments _____

_____

_____

Name of Recipe

_____

Name of Cookbook   *Page number*

_____

Date first prepared _____

Rate this recipe: *Excellent* ___ *Good* ___ *Average* ___

Additional Comments _____

_____

_____

Name of Recipe

_____

Name of Cookbook   *Page number*

_____

Date first prepared _____

Rate this recipe: Excellent ___ *Good* ___ *Average* ___

Additional Comments _____

_____

_____

_____

Name of Recipe

_____

Name of Cookbook   *Page number*

_____

Date first prepared _____

Rate this recipe: Excellent ___ *Good* ___ *Average* ___

Additional Comments _____

_____

_____

Name of Recipe

_____

Name of Cookbook   *Page number*

_____

Date first prepared _____

Rate this recipe: *Excellent* ____ *Good* ____ *Average* ____

Additional Comments _____

_____

_____

Name of Recipe

_____

Name of Cookbook   *Page number*

_____

Date first prepared _____

Rate this recipe: *Excellent* ____ *Good* ____ *Average* ____

Additional Comments _____

_____

_____

Name of Recipe

_____

Name of Cookbook   *Page number*

_____

Date first prepared _____

Rate this recipe: Excellent ___ *Good* ___ *Average* ___

Additional Comments _____

_____

_____

Name of Recipe

_____

Name of Cookbook   *Page number*

_____

Date first prepared _____

Rate this recipe: Excellent ___ *Good* ___ *Average* ___

Additional Comments _____

_____

_____

Seafood

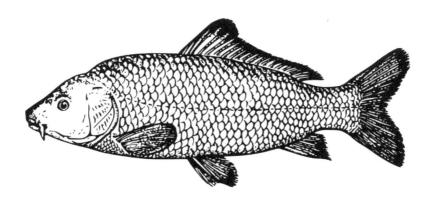

Name of Recipe   *Type of Seafood*

_____

Name of Cookbook   *Page number*

_____

Date first prepared _____

Rate this recipe: *Excellent* ____ *Good* ____ *Average* ____

Additional Comments _____

_____

_____

Name of Recipe   *Type of Seafood*

_____

Name of Cookbook   *Page number*

_____

Date first prepared _____

Rate this recipe: Excellent ____ *Good* ____ *Average*____

Additional Comments _____

_____

_____

Name of Recipe   *Type of Seafood*

_____

Name of Cookbook   *Page number*

_____

Date first prepared _____

Rate this recipe: Excellent ____ *Good* ____ *Average*____

Additional Comments _____

_____

_____

Name of Recipe   *Type of Seafood*

_____

Name of Cookbook   *Page number*

_____

Date first prepared _____

Rate this recipe: Excellent ____ *Good* ____ *Average* ____

Additional Comments _____

_____

_____

Name of Recipe   *Type of Seafood*

_____

Name of Cookbook   *Page number*

_____

Date first prepared _____

Rate this recipe: Excellent ____ *Good* ____ *Average* ____

Additional Comments _____

_____

_____

Name of Recipe   *Type of Seafood*

_____

Name of Cookbook   *Page number*

_____

Date first prepared _____

Rate this recipe: Excellent ___ *Good* ___ *Average* ___

Additional Comments _____

_____

_____

Name of Recipe   *Type of Seafood*

_____

Name of Cookbook   *Page number*

_____

Date first prepared _____

Rate this recipe: Excellent ___ *Good* ___ *Average* ___

Additional Comments _____

_____

_____

Name of Recipe   Type of Seafood

_____

Name of Cookbook   Page number

_____

Date first prepared _____

Rate this recipe: Excellent ____ Good ____ Average____

Additional Comments _____

_____

_____

Name of Recipe   Type of Seafood

_____

Name of Cookbook   Page number

_____

Date first prepared _____

Rate this recipe: Excellent ____ Good ____ Average____

Additional Comments _____

_____

_____

Name of Recipe   *Type of Seafood*

_____

Name of Cookbook   *Page number*

_____

Date first prepared _____

Rate this recipe: Excellent ____ *Good* ____ *Average* ____

Additional Comments _____

_____

_____

Name of Recipe   *Type of Seafood*

_____

Name of Cookbook   *Page number*

_____

Date first prepared _____

Rate this recipe: Excellent ____ *Good* ____ *Average* ____

Additional Comments _____

_____

_____

Name of Recipe　　　　　　　　*Type of Seafood*

_____

Name of Cookbook　　　　　　　*Page number*

_____

Date first prepared _____

Rate this recipe: Excellent ___ *Good* ___ *Average* ___

Additional Comments _____

_____

_____

Name of Recipe　　　　　　　　*Type of Seafood*

_____

Name of Cookbook　　　　　　　*Page number*

_____

Date first prepared _____

Rate this recipe: Excellent ___ *Good* ___ *Average* ___

Additional Comments _____

_____

_____

Name of Recipe   Type of Seafood

_____

Name of Cookbook   Page number

_____

Date first prepared _____

Rate this recipe: Excellent ____ Good ____ Average____

Additional Comments _____

_____

_____

Name of Recipe   Type of Seafood

_____

Name of Cookbook   Page number

_____

Date first prepared _____

Rate this recipe: Excellent ____ Good ____ Average____

Additional Comments _____

_____

_____

Name of Recipe   Type of Seafood

_____

Name of Cookbook   Page number

_____

Date first prepared _____

Rate this recipe: Excellent ____ Good ____ Average ____

Additional Comments _____

_____

_____

Name of Recipe   Type of Seafood

_____

Name of Cookbook   Page number

_____

Date first prepared _____

Rate this recipe: Excellent ____ Good ____ Average ____

Additional Comments _____

_____

_____

Other Meats

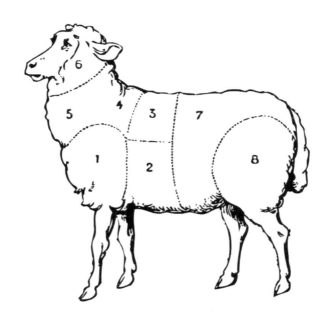

Name of Recipe   Type of Meat

_____

Name of Cookbook   Page number

_____

Date first prepared _____

Rate this recipe: Excellent ____ Good ____ Average ____

Additional Comments _____

_____

_____

Name of Recipe   *Type of Meat*

_____

Name of Cookbook   *Page number*

_____

Date first prepared _____

Rate this recipe: *Excellent* ____ *Good* ____ *Average*____

Additional Comments _____

_____

_____

Name of Recipe   *Type of Meat*

_____

Name of Cookbook   *Page number*

_____

Date first prepared _____

Rate this recipe: *Excellent* ____ *Good* ____ *Average*____

Additional Comments _____

_____

_____

Name of Recipe   *Type of Meat*

_____

Name of Cookbook   *Page number*

_____

Date first prepared _____

Rate this recipe: Excellent ___ *Good* ___ *Average* ___

Additional Comments _____

_____

_____

Name of Recipe   *Type of Meat*

_____

Name of Cookbook   *Page number*

_____

Date first prepared _____

Rate this recipe: Excellent ___ *Good* ___ *Average* ___

Additional Comments _____

_____

_____

Name of Recipe   *Type of Meat*

_____

Name of Cookbook   *Page number*

_____

Date first prepared _____

Rate this recipe: *Excellent* ___ *Good* ___ *Average* ___

Additional Comments _____

_____

_____

Name of Recipe   *Type of Meat*

_____

Name of Cookbook   *Page number*

_____

Date first prepared _____

Rate this recipe: *Excellent* ___ *Good* ___ *Average* ___

Additional Comments _____

_____

_____

Name of Recipe   Type of Meat

_____

Name of Cookbook   Page number

_____

Date first prepared _____

Rate this recipe: Excellent ____ Good ____ Average____

Additional Comments _____

_____

_____

Name of Recipe   Type of Meat

_____

Name of Cookbook   Page number

_____

Date first prepared _____

Rate this recipe: Excellent ____ Good ____ Average____

Additional Comments _____

_____

_____

Name of Recipe   *Type of Meat*

_____

Name of Cookbook   *Page number*

_____

Date first prepared _____

Rate this recipe: Excellent ___ Good ___ Average___

Additional Comments _____

_____

_____

Name of Recipe   *Type of Meat*

_____

Name of Cookbook   *Page number*

_____

Date first prepared _____

Rate this recipe: Excellent ___ Good ___ Average___

Additional Comments _____

_____

_____

Breads

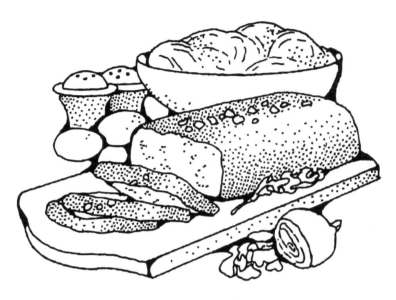

Name of Recipe

_____

Name of Cookbook   Page number

_____

Date first prepared _____

Rate this recipe: Excellent ____ Good ____ Average____

Additional Comments _____

_____

_____

Name of Recipe

_____

Name of Cookbook   *Page number*

_____

Date first prepared _____

Rate this recipe: Excellent ____ *Good* ____ *Average* ____

Additional Comments _____

_____

_____

Name of Recipe

_____

Name of Cookbook   *Page number*

_____

Date first prepared _____

Rate this recipe: Excellent ____ *Good* ____ *Average* ____

Additional Comments _____

_____

_____

Name of Recipe

_____

Name of Cookbook   Page number

_____

Date first prepared _____

Rate this recipe: Excellent ____ Good ____ Average____

Additional Comments _____

_____

_____

Name of Recipe

_____

Name of Cookbook   Page number

_____

Date first prepared _____

Rate this recipe: Excellent ____ Good ____ Average____

Additional Comments _____

_____

_____

Name of Recipe

_____

Name of Cookbook   Page number

_____

Date first prepared _____

Rate this recipe: Excellent ____ Good ____ Average____

Additional Comments _____

_____

_____

═══

Name of Recipe

_____

Name of Cookbook   Page number

_____

Date first prepared _____

Rate this recipe: Excellent ____ Good ____ Average____

Additional Comments _____

_____

_____

Name of Recipe

_____

Name of Cookbook   Page number

_____

Date first prepared _____

Rate this recipe: Excellent ____ Good ____ Average____

Additional Comments _____

_____

_____

Name of Recipe

_____

Name of Cookbook   Page number

_____

Date first prepared _____

Rate this recipe: Excellent ____ Good ____ Average____

Additional Comments _____

_____

_____

Name of Recipe

_____

Name of Cookbook   *Page number*

_____

Date first prepared _____

Rate this recipe: *Excellent* ___ *Good* ___ *Average* ___

Additional Comments _____

_____

_____

_____

━━

Name of Recipe

_____

Name of Cookbook   *Page number*

_____

Date first prepared _____

Rate this recipe: *Excellent* ___ *Good* ___ *Average* ___

Additional Comments _____

_____

_____

Name of Recipe

_____

Name of Cookbook   *Page number*

_____

Date first prepared _____

Rate this recipe: Excellent ____ *Good* ____ *Average* ____

Additional Comments _____

_____

_____

Name of Recipe

_____

Name of Cookbook   *Page number*

_____

Date first prepared _____

Rate this recipe: Excellent ____ *Good* ____ *Average* ____

Additional Comments _____

_____

_____

Name of Recipe

_____

Name of Cookbook   *Page number*

_____

Date first prepared _____

Rate this recipe: *Excellent* ____ *Good* ____ *Average* ____

Additional Comments _____

_____

_____

Name of Recipe

_____

Name of Cookbook   *Page number*

_____

Date first prepared _____

Rate this recipe: *Excellent* ____ *Good* ____ *Average* ____

Additional Comments _____

_____

_____

Name of Recipe

_____

Name of Cookbook   *Page number*

_____

Date first prepared _____

Rate this recipe: Excellent ____ *Good* ____ *Average* ____

Additional Comments _____

_____

_____

Name of Recipe

_____

Name of Cookbook   *Page number*

_____

Date first prepared _____

Rate this recipe: Excellent ____ *Good* ____ *Average* ____

Additional Comments _____

_____

_____

Name of Recipe

_____

Name of Cookbook   Page number

_____

Date first prepared _____

Rate this recipe: Excellent ____ Good ____ Average____

Additional Comments _____

_____

_____

Name of Recipe

_____

Name of Cookbook   Page number

_____

Date first prepared _____

Rate this recipe: Excellent ____ Good ____ Average____

Additional Comments _____

_____

_____

Desserts/Sweets

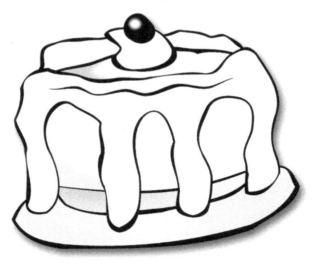

Name of Recipe

_____

Name of Cookbook   Page number

_____

Date first prepared _____

Rate this recipe: Excellent ____ Good ____ Average____

Additional Comments _____

_____

_____

Name of Recipe

_____

Name of Cookbook   *Page number*

_____

Date first prepared _____

Rate this recipe: *Excellent* ____ *Good* ____ *Average* ____

Additional Comments _____

_____

_____

═══

Name of Recipe

_____

Name of Cookbook   *Page number*

_____

Date first prepared _____

Rate this recipe: *Excellent* ____ *Good* ____ *Average* ____

Additional Comments _____

_____

_____

Name of Recipe

_____

Name of Cookbook   *Page number*

_____

Date first prepared _____

Rate this recipe: *Excellent* ____ *Good* ____ *Average* ____

Additional Comments _____

_____

_____

_____

Name of Recipe

_____

Name of Cookbook   *Page number*

_____

Date first prepared _____

Rate this recipe: *Excellent* ____ *Good* ____ *Average* ____

Additional Comments _____

_____

_____

Name of Recipe

_____

Name of Cookbook   *Page number*

_____

Date first prepared _____

Rate this recipe: *Excellent* ___ *Good* ___ *Average* ___

Additional Comments _____

_____

_____

Name of Recipe

_____

Name of Cookbook   *Page number*

_____

Date first prepared _____

Rate this recipe: *Excellent* ___ *Good* ___ *Average* ___

Additional Comments _____

_____

_____

Name of Recipe

_____

Name of Cookbook   *Page number*

_____

Date first prepared _____

Rate this recipe: Excellent ___ *Good* ___ *Average* ___

Additional Comments _____

_____

_____

Name of Recipe

_____

Name of Cookbook   *Page number*

_____

Date first prepared _____

Rate this recipe: Excellent ___ *Good* ___ *Average* ___

Additional Comments _____

_____

_____

Name of Recipe

_____

Name of Cookbook   *Page number*

_____

Date first prepared _____

Rate this recipe: *Excellent* ____ *Good* ____ *Average* ____

Additional Comments _____

_____

_____

Name of Recipe

_____

Name of Cookbook   *Page number*

_____

Date first prepared _____

Rate this recipe: *Excellent* ____ *Good* ____ *Average* ____

Additional Comments _____

_____

_____

Name of Recipe

_____

Name of Cookbook   *Page number*

_____

Date first prepared _____

Rate this recipe: Excellent ____ *Good* ____ *Average*____

Additional Comments _____

_____

_____

Name of Recipe

_____

Name of Cookbook   *Page number*

_____

Date first prepared _____

Rate this recipe: Excellent ____ *Good* ____ *Average*____

Additional Comments _____

_____

_____

Name of Recipe

_____

Name of Cookbook   .   Page number

_____

Date first prepared _____

Rate this recipe: Excellent ____ Good ____ Average____

Additional Comments _____

_____

_____

Name of Recipe

_____

Name of Cookbook   Page number

_____

Date first prepared _____

Rate this recipe: Excellent ____ Good ____ Average____

Additional Comments _____

_____

_____

Name of Recipe

_____

Name of Cookbook   Page number

_____

Date first prepared _____

Rate this recipe: Excellent ____ Good ____ Average____

Additional Comments _____

_____

_____

━━━━━━━━━━━━━━━━━━━━━━━━━━━━━

Name of Recipe

_____

Name of Cookbook   Page number

_____

Date first prepared _____

Rate this recipe: Excellent ____ Good ____ Average____

Additional Comments _____

_____

_____

Name of Recipe

_____

Name of Cookbook   Page number

_____

Date first prepared _____

Rate this recipe: Excellent ___ Good ___ Average ___

Additional Comments _____

_____

_____

Name of Recipe

_____

Name of Cookbook   Page number

_____

Date first prepared _____

Rate this recipe: Excellent ___ Good ___ Average ___

Additional Comments _____

_____

_____

Name of Recipe

_____

Name of Cookbook   *Page number*

_____

Date first prepared _____

Rate this recipe: Excellent ____ Good ____ Average____

Additional Comments _____

_____

_____

═══

Name of Recipe

_____

Name of Cookbook   *Page number*

_____

Date first prepared _____

Rate this recipe: Excellent ____ Good ____ Average____

Additional Comments _____

_____

_____

Name of Recipe

_____

Name of Cookbook   *Page number*

_____

Date first prepared _____

Rate this recipe: Excellent ____ Good ____ Average ____

Additional Comments _____

_____

_____

Name of Recipe

_____

Name of Cookbook   *Page number*

_____

Date first prepared _____

Rate this recipe: Excellent ____ Good ____ Average ____

Additional Comments _____

_____

_____

Name of Recipe

_____

Name of Cookbook   *Page number*

_____

Date first prepared _____

Rate this recipe: Excellent ____ *Good* ____ *Average* ____

Additional Comments _____

_____

_____

Name of Recipe

_____

Name of Cookbook   *Page number*

_____

Date first prepared _____

Rate this recipe: Excellent ____ *Good* ____ *Average* ____

Additional Comments _____

_____

_____

Name of Recipe

_____

Name of Cookbook   *Page number*

_____

Date first prepared _____

Rate this recipe: Excellent ___ *Good* ___ *Average* ___

Additional Comments _____

_____

_____

Name of Recipe

_____

Name of Cookbook   *Page number*

_____

Date first prepared _____

Rate this recipe: Excellent ___ *Good* ___ *Average* ___

Additional Comments _____

_____

_____

Name of Recipe

_____

Name of Cookbook   Page number

_____

Date first prepared _____

Rate this recipe: Excellent ____ Good ____ Average____

Additional Comments _____

_____

_____

Name of Recipe

_____

Name of Cookbook   Page number

_____

Date first prepared _____

Rate this recipe: Excellent ____ Good ____ Average____

Additional Comments _____

_____

_____

Name of Recipe

_____

Name of Cookbook   *Page number*

_____

Date first prepared _____

Rate this recipe: *Excellent* ___ *Good* ___ *Average* ___

Additional Comments _____

_____

_____

Name of Recipe

_____

Name of Cookbook   *Page number*

_____

Date first prepared _____

Rate this recipe: *Excellent* ___ *Good* ___ *Average* ___

Additional Comments _____

_____

_____

Name of Recipe

_____

Name of Cookbook   *Page number*

_____

Date first prepared _____

Rate this recipe: Excellent ____ Good ____ Average____

Additional Comments _____

_____

_____

Name of Recipe

_____

Name of Cookbook   *Page number*

_____

Date first prepared _____

Rate this recipe: Excellent ____ Good ____ Average____

Additional Comments _____

_____

_____

Name of Recipe

_____

Name of Cookbook   *Page number*

_____

Date first prepared _____

Rate this recipe: *Excellent* ___ *Good* ___ *Average* ___

Additional Comments _____

_____

_____

Name of Recipe

_____

Name of Cookbook   *Page number*

_____

Date first prepared _____

Rate this recipe: *Excellent* ___ *Good* ___ *Average* ___

Additional Comments _____

_____

_____

Name of Recipe

_____

Name of Cookbook   Page number

_____

Date first prepared _____

Rate this recipe: Excellent ____ Good ____ Average____

Additional Comments _____

_____

_____

Name of Recipe

_____

Name of Cookbook   Page number

_____

Date first prepared _____

Rate this recipe: Excellent ____ Good ____ Average____

Additional Comments _____

_____

_____

Name of Recipe

_____

Name of Cookbook   *Page number*

_____

Date first prepared _____

Rate this recipe: *Excellent* ___ *Good* ___ *Average*___

Additional Comments _____

_____

_____

═══

Name of Recipe

_____

Name of Cookbook   *Page number*

_____

Date first prepared _____

Rate this recipe: *Excellent* ___ *Good* ___ *Average*___

Additional Comments _____

_____

_____

Name of Recipe

_____

Name of Cookbook   *Page number*

_____

Date first prepared _____

Rate this recipe: Excellent ___ *Good* ___ *Average* ___

Additional Comments _____

_____

_____

_____

Name of Recipe

_____

Name of Cookbook   *Page number*

_____

Date first prepared _____

Rate this recipe: Excellent ___ *Good* ___ *Average* ___

Additional Comments _____

_____

_____

Specialty Drinks

Name of Recipe

_____

Name of Cookbook　　　　　　　　*Page number*

_____

Date first prepared _____

Rate this recipe: Excellent ____ *Good* ____ *Average* ____

Additional Comments _____

_____

_____

Name of Recipe

_____

Name of Cookbook   *Page number*

_____

Date first prepared _____

Rate this recipe: Excellent ____ *Good* ____ *Average* ____

Additional Comments _____

_____

_____

Name of Recipe

_____

Name of Cookbook   *Page number*

_____

Date first prepared _____

Rate this recipe: Excellent ____ *Good* ____ *Average* ____

Additional Comments _____

_____

_____

Name of Recipe

_____

Name of Cookbook   Page number

_____

Date first prepared _____

Rate this recipe: Excellent ____ Good ____ Average____

Additional Comments _____

_____

_____

Name of Recipe

_____

Name of Cookbook   Page number

_____

Date first prepared _____

Rate this recipe: Excellent ____ Good ____ Average____

Additional Comments _____

_____

_____

Name of Recipe

_____

Name of Cookbook   *Page number*

_____

Date first prepared _____

Rate this recipe: Excellent ___ Good ___ Average___

Additional Comments _____

_____

_____

Name of Recipe

_____

Name of Cookbook   *Page number*

_____

Date first prepared _____

Rate this recipe: Excellent ___ Good ___ Average___

Additional Comments _____

_____

_____

Name of Recipe

_____

Name of Cookbook   Page number

_____

Date first prepared _____

Rate this recipe: Excellent ____ Good ____ Average ____

Additional Comments _____

_____

_____

═══

Name of Recipe

_____

Name of Cookbook   Page number

_____

Date first prepared _____

Rate this recipe: Excellent ____ Good ____ Average ____

Additional Comments _____

_____

_____

Name of Recipe

_____

Name of Cookbook   *Page number*

_____

Date first prepared _____

Rate this recipe: Excellent ____ *Good* ____ *Average* ____

Additional Comments _____

_____

_____

Name of Recipe

_____

Name of Cookbook   *Page number*

_____

Date first prepared _____

Rate this recipe: Excellent ____ *Good* ____ *Average* ____

Additional Comments _____

_____

_____

CPSIA information can be obtained
at www.ICGtesting.com
Printed in the USA
FSHW021959100621
82305FS